WHO'S COUNTING?

NANCY TAFURI

A MULBERRY PAPERBACK BOOK • NEW YORK

FOR ADA

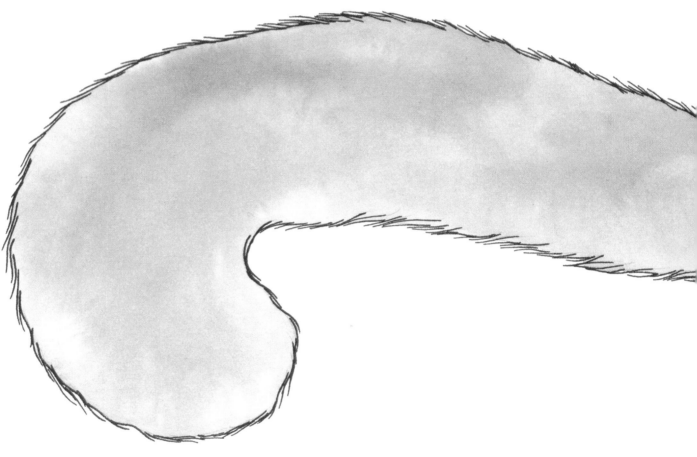

A black line was combined with watercolor paints for the full-color illustrations. The text type is ITC Weiderman.

Printed in the United States of America.

First Mulberry Edition, 1993.

10 9 8 7 6 5 4 3 2 1

Library of Congress Cataloging-in-Publication Data
Tafuri, Nancy.   Who's counting?
Summary: Text and illustrations of a variety of animals introduce the numbers one through ten.
1. Counting—Juvenile literature.
[1. Counting]   I. Title.
QA113.T34   1993   513.2'11 —dc20
ISBN 0-688-12266-3
92-24604 CIP AC

1 SQUIRREL

2 BIRDS

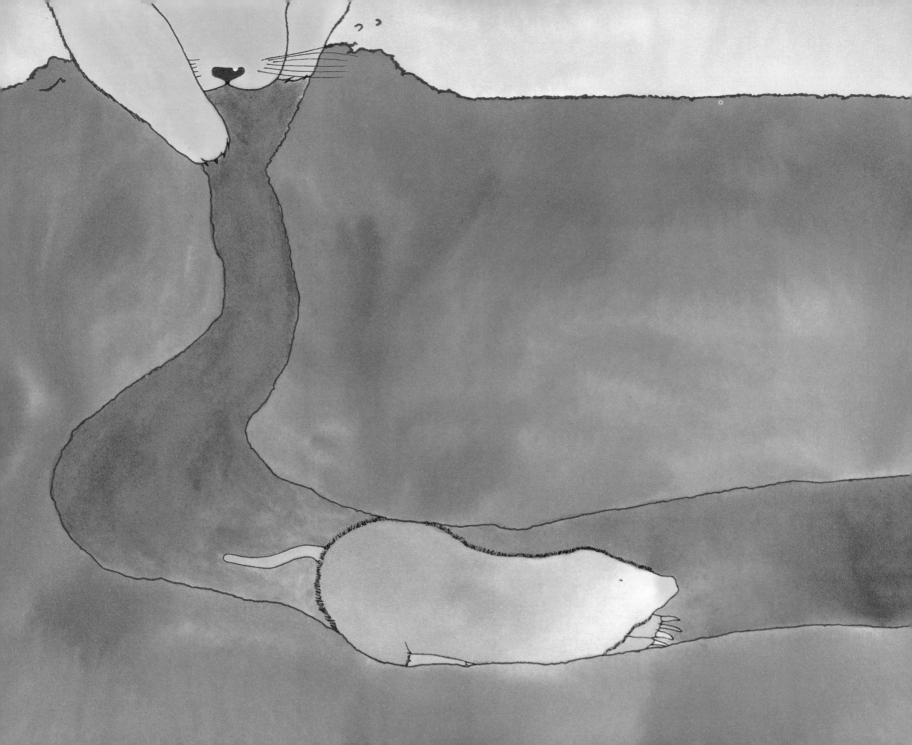

3 MOLES

4 GEESE

5
EGGS

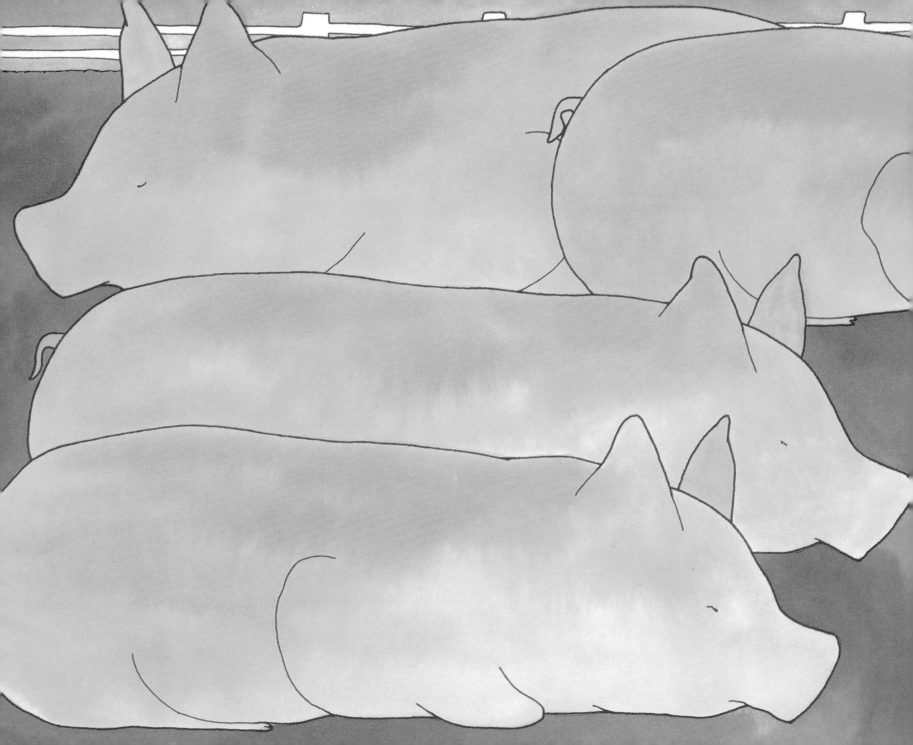

6 PIGLETS

7 RABBITS

8

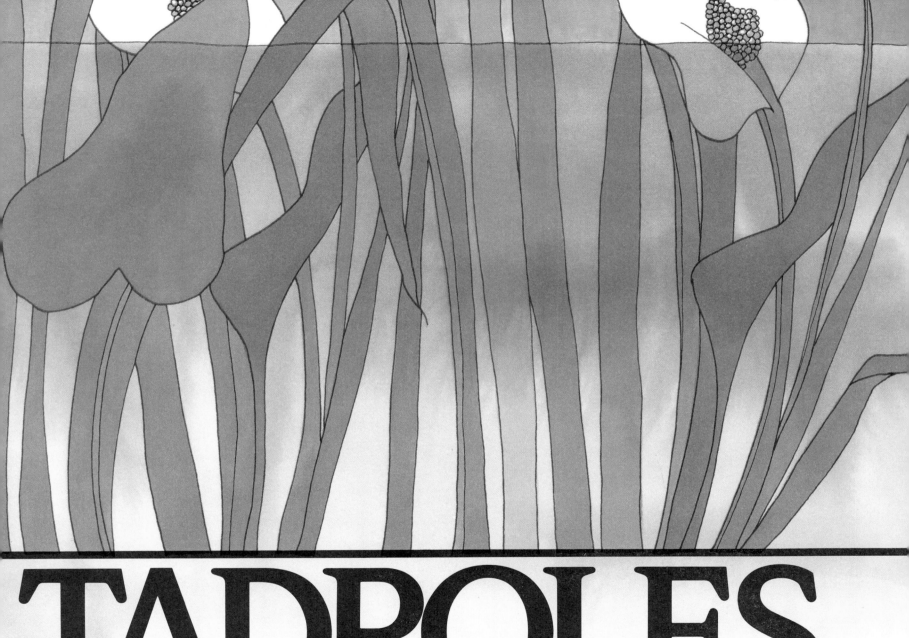

TADPOLES

9 FLOWERS

AND

10 PUPPIES-

EATING!